Th sci nc in...

...a pair of
GLASSES

The science of light and more...

Brian Williams

W
FRANKLIN WATTS
LONDON•SYDNEY

First published in 2008
by Franklin Watts

Copyright © Franklin Watts 2008

Franklin Watts
338 Euston Road
London NW1 3BH

Franklin Watts Australia
Level 17/207 Kent Street
Sydney, NSW 2000

Planning and production by
Discovery Books Limited
Editor: Rebecca Hunter
Designer: Keith Williams
Illustrator: Stefan Chabluk
Photo researcher: Rachel Tisdale

Every attempt has been made to
clear copyright. Should there be any
inadvertent omission please apply to
the publisher for rectification.

Dewey number 535

ISBN 978 0 7496 8237 8

Printed in China

Franklin Watts is a division of Hachette
Children's Books, an Hachette Livre UK
company. www.hachettelivre.co.uk

Photo acknowledgements: Getty Images/Robin Lynne Gibson, front cover top; istockphoto.com, front cover bottom left; istockphoto.com/Zsolt Nyulaszi, front cover bottom right; istockphoto.com/Jane Norton, p. 4; istockphoto.com/Ben Blankenburg, p. 5; istockphoto.com/Sunagotov Dmitry, p. 6; Getty Images/Charles Gupton/Stone, p. 9; istockphoto.com/Rui Matos, p. 11; Corbis, p. 13; istockphoto.com, p. 14; Getty Images/Hulton Archive, p. 15; Corbis/Michael A. Keller, p. 16; istockphoto.com/Jodie Coston, p. 18; Corbis/Jim Craigmyle, p. 19; istockphoto.com/Liza McCorkle, p. 20; Corbis/Charles Gupton, p. 21; Corbis/Hulton-Deutsch Collection, p. 22; Corbis/Alan Schein Photography, p. 23; istockphoto.com/Marcin Stalmach, p. 24; Corbis/Steve Marcus/Reuters, p. 25; istockphoto.com, p. 26 & 27 top; Corbis/Roger Ressmeyer, p. 27 bottom; Getty Images/David Deas/DK Stock, p. 28; Getty Images/National Geographic, p. 29 top; istockphoto.com, p. 29 bottom

Contents

Words that appear in **bold**
are in the glossary on page 30.

Why wear glasses?

Glasses allow people with impaired vision to read more easily and see distant objects more clearly. How? It's all to do with light and lenses.

What makes a pair of glasses?

Glasses look simple – two bits of glass, or more usually nowadays clear plastic, set in a frame. Each bit of plastic is a lens. The frame has two arms, called temples. A centre rest (bridge) with pads grips the nose lightly. The arms are hinged so the glasses can be folded away in a case.

▼ *The two main parts of a pair of glasses are the frame and the lenses.*

Why do some people need glasses?

Eyesight tends to get worse as we get older, but some children may need glasses too. Studies show that around 20 per cent of children are short-sighted or long-sighted (see pages 12-13). Glasses are not always needed to correct eye problems in childhood, and some children who wear glasses no longer need them when they are grown-up.

▼ *Wearing glasses helps many people read more easily.*

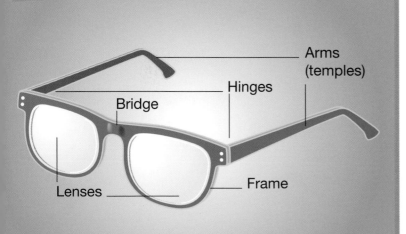

Arms (temples)

Hinges

Bridge

Lenses

Frame

▲ *These skiers wear sunglasses to shield their eyes from the dazzling glare of sunlit snow.*

A sight test shows if a person needs glasses. An expert optician carries out this test. After checking each eye, the optician decides what lens is required and writes a **prescription**, like a doctor writes a prescription for medicines. Lenses of the correct strength are fitted into a frame chosen by the wearer.

Eye protection

People also wear glasses to protect their eyes. Sunglasses filter out bright sunshine and glare from reflective surfaces such as snow. Safety glasses, goggles and **visors** shield the eyes from damage at work or play – such as when spray-painting, handling chemicals, cutting metal, skiing or motorcycling.

What is light?

With or without glasses, we need light to see. Light is a form of energy given off by the Sun and other stars. All light comes from atoms giving off energy – the atoms can be in anything from a star to a lighted match.

Natural light comes from the Sun, stars, or insects such as fireflies, and can't be controlled by people. Artificial light, from an electric lamp, a candle, or a laser, can be controlled by people.

What's light made of?

Light travels as **rays**, made up of tiny **particles** called photons. It travels in straight lines. You can see this by switching on a torch. When you shine a torch into a dark room, the beam of light seems to hit the wall instantly. Nothing travels faster than light. The speed of light is 300,000 km per second.

Seeing through things

A lens must be transparent, to let light rays through without mixing or 'scattering' them. If you stick parcel tape over one lens of a pair of glasses, it's like having one eye closed. A sheet of tracing paper lets some light through, but the rays get mixed up so that you

NEVER look directly at the Sun; it is so bright it can damage your eyes.

◀ *A glowing red sunset. The Sun is a star, a ball of very hot gas that gives off light.*

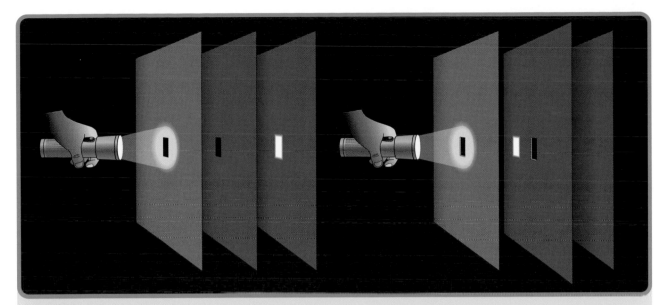

▲ *Here's how to prove light travels in a straight line. Take two sheets of card. Make the same-sized hole in the middle of each sheet. If you line up the holes and shine a torch through the first hole, a beam of light will pass straight through the other hole. If the holes are not lined up – light will not shine through the second hole.*

can't see clearly through the paper. The paper is **translucent**. Light can't pass through a brick wall or a wooden door, because brick and wood are **opaque** – they block light rays.

Solar energy

Sunglasses stop our eyes from being dazzled by the Sun. Even at a distance of 150 million km from the Earth, the Sun is incredibly bright. Nuclear reactions inside the Sun generate huge amounts of light, heat and other forms of energy, which speed across space as **radiation**. As well as heat and light, the Sun gives off radio waves, **ultraviolet rays** and **X-rays**.

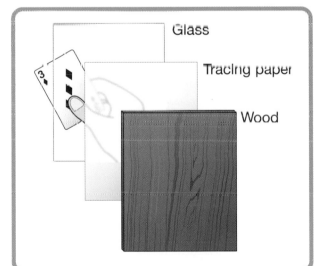

Glass

Tracing paper

Wood

▲ *Glass is transparent, so light passes through easily (you can see the playing card clearly). Tracing paper is translucent – some light gets through. Wood is opaque – no light gets through.*

Seeing things

We use our eyes all the time – reading, working, watching DVDs, playing games. Sight provides about half of all the information that enters the brain.

Light enters the transparent front of the eye (the **cornea**), and is focused by a lens onto a screen (the **retina**). Light-sensitive cells send nerve signals to the brain, and we 'see' a picture.

Reflections

Our eyes are bombarded by light from all around. Whenever light hits an obstacle, it bounces off in another direction. This is **reflection**. Everything – a desk, your hand, this page in the book – reflects light.

Discovering the lens

The ancient Greeks studied the eye 2,500 years ago. Later, Arab scientists discovered that vision had to do with light and the way light bends. In the Middle Ages (800s–1400s), scientists in the Middle East and Europe experimented with shaped glass (a lens) to make things look bigger or 'magnified'. In the 1200s, the English scientist Roger Bacon sent a magnifying glass to Pope Clement IV in Rome, to help him read more easily.

◄ *You can use a mirror to peer around a door. The mirror reflects light rays towards your eye, so you see an **image** of the object (in this case the cat on the other side of the door).*

If the light from an object reaches our eyes, we see an image. For people who need them, glasses make sure that the image is clear, whether it's a page of text close up or a mountain on the far horizon.

▼ *Glasses can't make the funny images we see in a 'crazy mirror' look normal. The curved glass in this kind of mirror scatters light rays so the image is distorted. We look taller, or fatter or just weird.*

Mirrors

Thousands of years ago, people discovered that a smooth, shiny surface (such as polished metal) reflects light. It acts as a mirror because it reflects light in one direction. A rough surface scatters the light in all directions. So you can see your face in a glass mirror (smooth), but not in a sheet of paper (which is rough, even if it looks smooth).

How do my eyes work?

The eye is a ball of fluid, with a transparent front (the cornea) which lets in light. The pupil in the centre of the iris (the coloured area of the eye) widens or narrows to let in more or less light.

Inside the eye is a pea-sized lens. This is flexible and moved by tiny muscles to adjust the **focus**, in the same way that you change the focus on a pair of binoculars. The lens bends light entering the eye and focuses an image on the retina, the layer inside the eye that contains light-sensitive cells.

From eye to brain

The image on the retina is upside down, because of the way the light rays are bent. The retina changes the image into nerve-signals, which speed along the optic nerve to the brain. The brain changes the signals back to a picture, the right way up. It all happens in a flash.

▼ *This is what happens inside your eye. Light reflected off an object (the pear) enters the eye and produces an (upside-down) image at the back of the eye.*

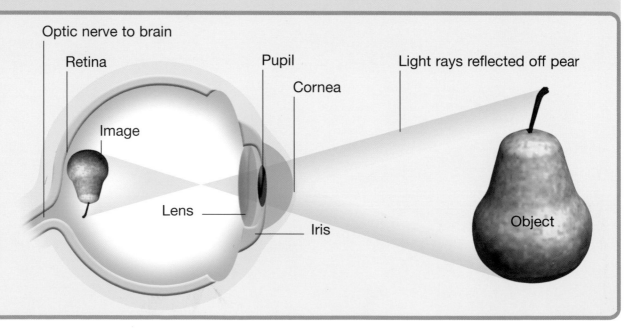

Optic nerve to brain

Retina

Pupil

Cornea

Light rays reflected off pear

Image

Lens

Iris

Object

How the eye focuses

Light rays from objects some distance away enter the eye almost parallel. The rays are bent slightly towards one another by the lens, to form an image. Light rays from objects close to the eye spread apart, and so the lens has to bend them more, to focus a sharp image.

Failure to focus is a common vision problem. The lenses in glasses help the lenses in the eyes to focus properly.

Two eyes better than one?

Humans, and some animals, have two, forward-facing eyes. This is 'binocular vision'. Each eye gives a slightly different image of the same object. This helps when judging distance. So in animals, two eyes are better than one for climbing, jumping and hunting for food. Humans can see quite well with just one eye though, and many people have one eye that's naturally slightly weaker than the other.

▼ Owls have very large, forward-facing eyes, and most owls can see better than we can at night. Like people, owls have binocular vision, so when hunting, an owl sees a mouse with both eyes at the same time. An owl has to turn its head to look sideways, whereas people have fairly good all-round vision.

Seeing clearly

When we're young, most people's eyes make clear images unaided. As we get older, most of us will need glasses.

Short-sight and long-sight

Two common vision weaknesses are short-sight and long-sight. If a person is short-sighted, things close up look clear, but objects further away look blurred. The technical name for this condition is myopia. If someone is long-sighted, they see distant objects clearly but may have trouble reading small print in a book. This is hyperopia, also known as hypermetropia.

By middle age (40–50), most people experience presbyopia. With age, the lens of the eye gets less flexible. It can't adjust easily for objects close to and far away. Older people need glasses for reading, computer use, sewing and other close work.

Seeing colours

In the retina of the eye are two types of light-sensitive cell called rods and cones. Rods pick up light, but not colour. Cones are good at spotting

▼ These diagrams show the difference between short-sight and long-sight. Light rays entering the eye focus in front of the retina (short-sight) or beyond it (long-sight). The place where the rays meet is called the focal point.

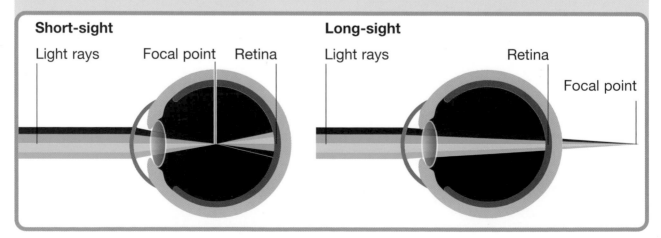

Short-sight

Light rays   Focal point   Retina

Long-sight

Light rays   Retina   Focal point

▲ *This photo of US soldiers making a parachute jump at night was taken using a night-vision device.*

Seeing in the dark

Ordinary glasses won't help you see in the dark. Night-vision aids used by soldiers are electronic devices with an inbuilt screen. They turn light into electric signals, boost the signals (to make them stronger), then turn them back to light. The result: the soldier sees a near-daylight picture.

colour, but don't work at night. At night, the rods work, but we see things mostly as white, black, or grey.

▶ *This diagram shows a cross-section of the retina. It contains two types of light-sensitive cell, rods and cones. These send messages to the brain through the optic nerve.*

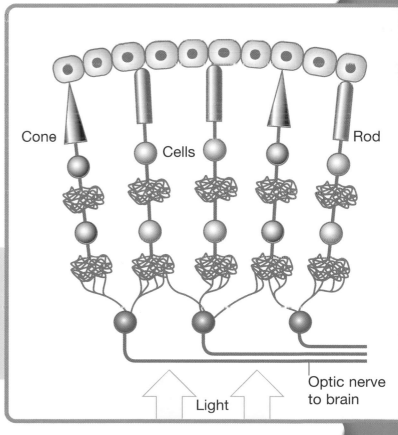

Cone

Cells

Rod

Light

Optic nerve to brain

A lens bends light

In glasses, it's the lens that makes the difference. Lenses are used in telescopes, cameras and microscopes. The magnifying glass you use to look at a bug in the grass has a lens too. There are lots of kinds of lenses.

Bendy light

A lens bends light. Light bends naturally when it passes from one substance to another – for example, from air through glass or water. You can see this by looking into clear water in a shallow pond or a fish tank. Try poking a stone at the bottom with a stick. You'll probably miss first time. The stone isn't quite where it appears to be. The stick seems to bend, at the point it enters the water. As the light passes from air to water, it bends. The scientific word for this is **refraction**. The strength of a lens is called its refractive (bending) power.

▼ *A magnifying glass has a lens that makes things look bigger. The lens can also distort the image slightly.*

◀ *This diagram shows how light can play tricks on our eyes. The pencil seems to bend at the point where it enters the water.*

Lenses for all reasons

Lenses are used in other things apart from glasses. The lenses in an **optical** microscope can magnify objects up to 2,000 times. The first microscope invented in 1590 had just one lens and had to be held close to the eye. Lenses in telescopes and binoculars help you see things that are far away.

How a lens works

A lens bends light rays passing through it. In a 'single-focus' lens all light rays passing through the lens meet at one point – the focal point. Depending on how it's made, the lens can make images bigger or smaller. An optician decides what shape and strength lens a person needs in their glasses. The most common kinds of lenses in glasses are convex lenses and concave lenses.

▶ *This is an early microscope, made by Robert Hooke in about 1670. To its left is the oil lamp and water-filled flask this British scientist used to light the specimens he was peering at.*

Convex and concave

Most lenses in glasses are either convex or concave, on one side or both. The lenses are made of glass or tough plastic. Plastic is lighter than glass, but scratches more easily. Polycarbonate lenses are extra-tough and hard to break.

Convex lenses

A convex lens is thicker in the middle than at the edges. This shape bends light inwards, making a virtual image that appears bigger. Glasses with convex lenses are worn by people who are long-sighted. The lens magnifies or enlarges objects close to the eyes, such as the words on the page of a book. Convex lenses are commonly used in reading glasses.

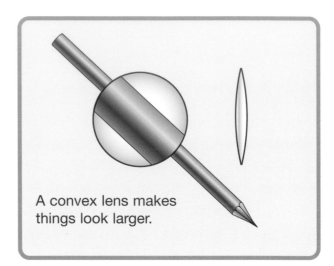

A convex lens makes things look larger.

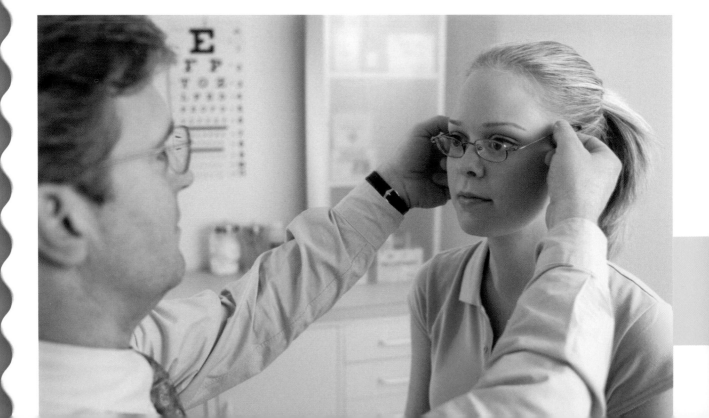

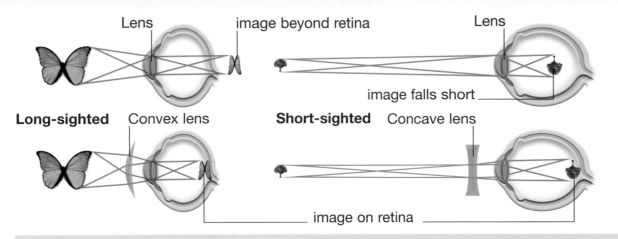

Lens | image beyond retina | Lens

Long-sighted | Convex lens | image falls short | **Short-sighted** | Concave lens

image on retina

> ▲ *Long-sighted people have trouble seeing objects up close. This is because the eye focuses most objects beyond the retina. This can be corrected with a convex lens. Short-sighted people have trouble seeing objects in the distance. This is because the eye focuses most objects short of the retina. This problem can be corrected with a concave lens.*

Concave lenses

A concave lens produces an image that looks smaller. This type of lens is thinner in the middle than at the edges. It bends light outwards. Glasses with concave lenses correct the vision of people who are short-sighted. The lens gives a clearer image of things at a distance, making them look less blurred.

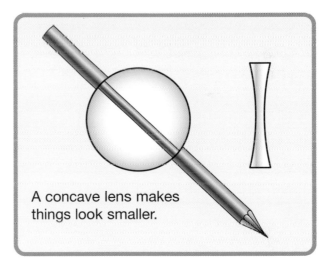

A concave lens makes things look smaller.

Tip: To remember the difference between 'convex' and 'concave', think of a cave. A concave lens is hollowed out, like a cave.

◄ *An optician helps a person choose new glasses, makes sure the lenses are the correct type, and that the glasses fit comfortably.*

A lens can start a fire

Concave lenses are also called diverging lenses – they bend parallel light rays away from one another. Convex lenses are called converging lenses – they bend light rays towards one another. By concentrating sunlight at its focal point, a convex lens can set light to a piece of paper. A forest fire can start from a discarded glass drinks bottle that acts as a lens. So take care.

Going to the optician

Many people today have their eyes checked regularly. In the past, people with eye problems or failing sight had little help from doctors. The eye and how we see were not clearly understood.

The first glasses

People first wore glasses more than 600 years ago. Glasses or 'spectacles' were held in the hand or stuck on the nose. The first 'modern' glasses with temple frames, worn as we wear glasses today, were made in Britain by Edward Scarlett in 1728. By then, eye doctors knew enough to prescribe different-strength lenses, but glasses were often sold by untrained traders. Poor people often wore second-hand glasses. Many still do.

Eye tests

If you find that the words in a book look fuzzy or a sign across the street is hard to read, it's time you visited the optician for an eye check-up. During an eye examination the optician will ask you to read lines of letters from a chart. He or she will check on distance vision (for car driving and watching TV), near vision (for reading) and intermediate vision (for computer use).

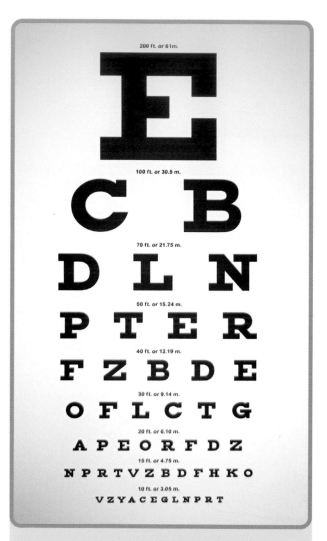

200 ft. or 61m.

E

100 ft. or 30.5 m.

C B

70 ft. or 21.75 m.

D L N

50 ft. or 15.24 m.

P T E R

40 ft. or 12.19 m.

F Z B D E

30 ft. or 9.14 m.

O F L C T G

20 ft. or 6.10 m.

A P E O R F D Z

15 ft. or 4.75 m.

N P R T V Z B D F H K O

10 ft. or 3.05 m.

V Z Y A C E G L N P R T

▲ *A sight-testing chart has the biggest letters at the top. The letters get smaller as you read down the lines, making it harder to read them.*

▲ *A young person has her vision tested with a **phoropter**. This device can be adjusted so the optician can decide what type and strength of lenses each person needs.*

He or she also checks to make sure both eyes are working together. Machines test how well the eyes focus and whether or not the field of vision (the area each eye covers) is normal. Using an **ophthalmoscope**, the optician looks into each eye closely, making sure that all is well and checks for conditions such as **glaucoma**.

The eye experts

The optician carrying out an eye examination may be an ophthalmologist or an optometrist. The main difference is that an opthalmologist and an optometrist undergo different forms of training. However, both may prescribe glasses, which are made and sold at the optician's surgery.

Correcting vision

Regular eye tests can help correct common vision problems, like astigmatism. One in three children aged 5-17, and most adults, have a slight astigmatism. It can be present at birth, or develop in later life.

What causes astigmatism?

Astigmatism happens when the cornea, at the front of the eye, is rippled or distorted, instead of being a smooth curve. Light entering the eye can't be focused properly, so the image is out of focus. Letters on a page look 'stretched' or smudged. An ordinary magnifying lens just makes the smudginess larger.

▼ *During an eye examination the optician uses a device to look closely at the outside and inside of the eye, as well as test vision. Testing at an early stage can show if a child needs glasses or not.*

Astigmatism

Light rays — Imperfect cornea — Retina

Normal eye

Light rays — Cornea with smooth curve — Retina

Astigmatism is corrected by wearing glasses with cylindrical lenses that change magnification according to their position, to focus light on one spot on the retina. The result is a clear image. Some people find cylinder lenses cause slight distortion, but this can be solved by adjusting the lenses.

Why do some people squint?

Strabismus or 'cross-eye' (also called a squint) happens when one eye is fixed on one object, and the other eye fixed on another. Normally, both eyes are turned towards the same object. Strabismus can occur in children. It is corrected by wearing glasses fitted with a **prism**, which pull the eyes gently and gradually into correct alignment.

◄ In astigmatism, not all the light rays from an object meet at one point, causing blurred vision. This can be corrected with a cylindrical lens.

Women's sight

Five hundred years ago, doctors thought women needed stronger lenses in their glasses than men. They gave two reasons. 1) Women were the 'weaker sex', and so had weaker eyes. 2) Women did more delicate work, such as sewing. In fact, there is no difference between women's and men's sight.

Glasses for all uses

Before the 1900s, all lenses in glasses were made of glass. They are now made of plastic because it is cheaper and breaks less easily.

The frames

Early glasses were often fixed to the nose with a clip (and called pince-nez, French for 'pinch-nose'), or even taped to a hat. Frames were made of bone, cow horn, wood, and even leather. Today, most frames are made of plastic, or from light but strong metals such as titanium, beryllium or aluminium.

The side-arms or temples have a wire core added inside, for strength.

The lenses

The lenses are fitted in the frame so that the **optical centre** of each lens is directly over the pupil of the eye. Lenses can be coated to make them scratch-resistant. They may also be tinted to filter out some sunlight and ultraviolet rays.

Bifocals

Reading glasses have 'single-vision' lenses. **Bifocal** glasses have lenses that have two sections of differing strength. They are useful when a person needs two or more different prescriptions – say, one for distance and another for reading. The wearer

◀ *Irish politician Timothy Healey (1855-1931) wearing pince-nez glasses. These glasses just sit on the nose, they are not attached to the ears.*

needs only one pair of glasses, not two. A trifocal lens has a third, medium-strength lens. In a progressive or varifocal lens, the focal-length changes gradually from the top of the lens to the bottom, with no visible division.

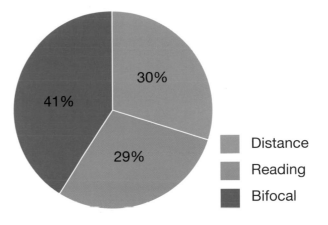

30%

41%

29%

Distance
Reading
Bifocal

Franklin's brainwave

In 1784, American politician and scientist Benjamin Franklin got fed up with having two pairs of glasses (for reading and long-distance). He made the first bifocals. He cut two pairs of spectacles (one for close vision, one for distance) in half across the lenses. He then stuck the two half-lenses together to make his bifocal glasses. The upper lens was helpful for far vision, the lower lens for close vision such as reading.

▲ *This pie chart shows how people use glasses – for reading, or for distance vision and also what proportion of glasses wearers wear bifocals.*

▼ *This modern statue of Benjamin Franklin, by George Lundeen, is in Philadelphia, USA. Franklin is wearing his trademark bifocal glasses.*

Contact lenses

Some people don't like wearing glasses. Contact lenses are the alternative to glasses. These lenses sit on the eye itself.

What are contact lenses?

A contact lens is a thin disc of plastic inserted between the eyeball and the eyelid. It's usually impossible to tell if someone is wearing contact lenses. They are useful for people who need to wear glasses most of the time.

Many athletes wear contact lenses; ordinary glasses can get steamed up with sweat, misted over by rain, or knocked off.

▼ *Contact lenses are inserted using the finger. Most contact-wearers soon get used to slipping the tiny lens in and out.*

▲ *Making a statement. Rap and hip-hop star Coolio chooses coloured contact lenses (and fangs) for a music awards ceremony. Film and TV actors can wear coloured lenses to produce a scary eye effect.*

The first contacts

The first contact lenses were made by a German eye doctor named Adolf Fick in 1887, though the idea had been put forward by others before him. His glass contacts were heavy and uncomfortable. Things improved for contact-wearers in the 1930s with the first plastic contact lens, moulded to fit the eye. Unfortunately, the lens had to be taken out frequently, since it blocked the natural flow of tears.

Modern contact lenses

A contact lens floats on a thin layer of tears, on the surface of the cornea. It is curved and focuses light on to the retina. Modern contact lenses are 'gas-permeable'. This means they 'breathe', letting oxygen reach the eye to keep the cornea healthy. Contacts can be single-focal or bifocal. Some people wear a short-sight lens in one eye, and a long-sight lens in the other.

A variety of contacts

Hard contacts (in use since the 1950s) are made of rigid plastic. Soft contacts (introduced in the 1970s) absorb moisture, so are more flexible. Many people find soft contacts more comfortable to wear. Contact lenses must be **sterilized** regularly. Disposable contacts do not need sterilizing, but are replaced every few days – some can be worn for up to two weeks.

Eye protection

Some people wear sunglasses or shades, even when there's no sunshine. Sunglasses have a useful purpose, to protect the eyes from bright sunlight or reflected glare (from snow, for instance).

Tinted glasses

Tinted glasses have photochromic lenses (coloured lenses); grey works well but you can buy other tints. These lenses darken your view outdoors (when struck by the ultraviolet rays in sunlight) to take away the brightness, but indoors they work just like ordinary glasses.

▼ *Sunglasses have become fashion items, but they can also be important in maintaining good eye health.*

Polarized and mirror-coated glasses

Normal light vibrates in all directions. Polarized light vibrates in one direction. In some sunglasses, a vertical polarizing plastic filter lets through only light rays vibrating in one direction (see diagram). The filter blocks horizontal rays of light – so reducing dazzle from sunlight reflected off smooth, flat surfaces, such as a road or water.

Mirror-coated sunglasses also block glare from the sun. Their lenses contain tiny mirrors that reflect sunlight away from the eye, to reduce glare.

▼ *The polarized lenses in sunglasses filter out some of the rays in sunlight, and so cut down glare.*

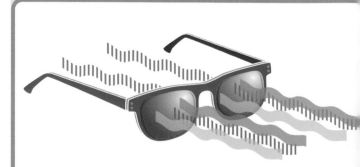

▲ Scientists should always wear protective safety glasses when doing experiments in the laboratory.

Safety glasses

Safety glasses will not shatter if struck by a flying object or a white-hot spark. Many people wear some form of eye protection at work – doctors (against blood-spatter), welders (against sparks and metal fragments) and DIY enthusiasts when using spray-paints, sanders, drills and other tools.

Extreme visors

The most effective safety glasses are a wraparound style, which provide protection both at front and side. The face visors worn by racing drivers and astronauts similarly provide complete face cover. The visor protects the eyes from heat, chemicals or impact. Astronauts need sun visors to shield them from the blinding sunlight in space.

▶ An astronaut is protected from the glaring sunlight in space by a gold-tinted visor fitted in the spacesuit helmet. The visor works like two-way glass. It reflects incoming light, but gives the astronaut a clear view.

Seeing is believing

The human eye is superbly adapted for what it has to do, but modern life puts new demands on it. Prehistoric people used their eyes mainly for hunting and finding food – adjusting from short to long-range vision all the time.

Today, many people use their eyes for hours at close range (while working on computers, playing games or watching TV). A person who sits in front of a screen all day is using his or her eyes very differently from a Stone Age hunter!

▼ *Full marks to all of you who take good care of your eyes! They should last you a lifetime.*

Look after your eyes

Eye care should begin when young. As a teenager, you may not need glasses for homework or computer gaming, but eye protection is advisable in some sports such as squash, and for craft or DIY activities.

Our eyes begin working together when we are babies only a few weeks old, and if we are lucky, go on working for the rest of our lives.

Glasses, glasses...

1 More than 100 million Americans wear glasses.
2 In Britain, more than 25 million people need glasses – about 3 million wear contact lenses.
3 Most opinion polls suggest that people think rimless glasses are 'more sexy' than those with rims.
4 The jobs people most associate with wearing glasses are 1) Librarian, 2) Teacher, 3) Lawyer.
5 Three out of four people under 40 who wear glasses do so because of short-sightedness.

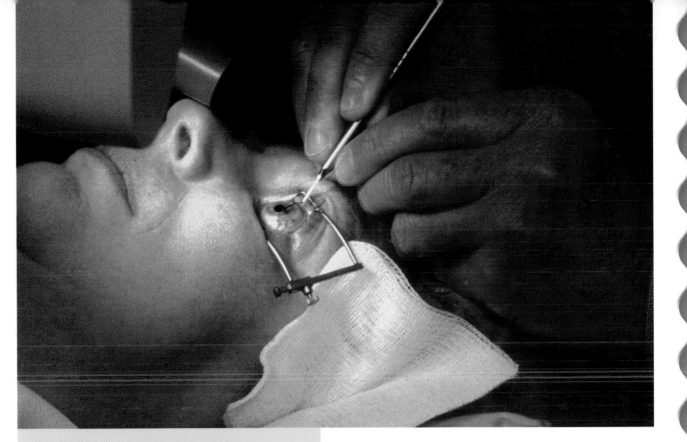

▲ An eye surgeon carries out delicate treatment of a patient's eye.

However, as we grow older, our eyesight does slowly get worse and the majority of us will end up needing glasses.

Science can now do amazing things to improve and save eyesight. Short-sightedness and long-sightedness can be corrected with laser surgery to save people wearing lenses. Doctors can graft a donor cornea into someone else's eye, for example, and **cataract** operations are now routine. What of the future? Throwaway virtual reality glasses? Eye implants? Glasses that see through walls? Who knows!

▲ In laser surgery the surgeon prepares the eyes for the laser by removing the top layer of cells – these will regrow or can be put back. A red beam then **vaporizes** tissue in the cornea to reshape it and correct the problem.

Glossary

atoms tiny particles from which things are made

bifocals glasses with lenses with two different strengths

cataract a condition affecting the lens in the eye, making it cloudy, and reducing vision

cornea the clear, outer covering of the eye

energy a force that makes things move or work; such as heat, light and electricity

focus the point where light rays come together after being refracted

glaucoma an eye condition that can lead to loss of sight

image the picture formed through a lens or when light is reflected

lens a material that can bring light rays closer together or bend them farther apart

opaque not able to be seen through

ophthalmoscope an instrument with a light and mirrors for examining the back of the eye and the lens

optical having to do with the eye

optical centre the part of a lens that has the strongest light-bending power

particle an extremely small part of something

phoropter an instrument used to test the eyes and check what strength lens a person needs in their glasses

polycarbonate a tough kind of plastic used to make 'unbreakable' glasses

prescription a written order for glasses or medicine

prism a kind of lens like a triangular block that can separate light into the colours of the rainbow

radiation the transfer of energy as electromagnetic waves or rays, such as light

ray a beam of light or other energy

reflection the bouncing back of light when it hits a surface

refraction the bending of light as it passes from one substance to another

retina the lining on the back wall of the eyeball that receives images

sterilize make free from bacteria

translucent allowing light, but not detailed shapes to pass through

ultraviolet rays invisible form of light from the Sun; they cause sunburn and can be harmful to unprotected eyes

vaporize convert a solid or a liquid into vapour

visors wraparound eye protectors, often built into headgear

X-rays a form of light from the Sun; these rays can pass through many materials that are opaque to normal light

Fu. th r info. m tion

Websites

www.antiquespectacles.com

This site contains information about the history of eye glasses, a timeline, pictures showing glasses through the ages, people in history who wore glasses and some fun games, too. It also tells you about the development of modern glasses.

www.college-optometrists.org

This site is mainly for those considering a career in eye-health. It contains information about 21st century eye-related technology and the training of eye doctors.

www.acept.asu.edu/PiN.act/ activities

This site has suggestions for light-related activities, such as simple experiments with mirrors and lenses to explore reflection, refraction and so on.

www.valemount.com/joel/ lightoptics

This is a science website, for students, teachers and parents, dedicated to light and optics studies. It deals with lots of different aspects of the way we see the world such as colour, lenses, the eye, and optical illusions.

www.health.learninginfo.org/ history_of_sunglasses

Here is more information about the history of sunglasses.

Note to parents and teachers: *Every effort has been made by the publishers to ensure that these websites are suitable for children, that they are of the highest educational value, and that they contain no inappropriate or offensive material. However, because of the nature of the Internet, it is impossible to guarantee that the contents of these sites will not be altered. We strongly advise that Internet access is supervised by a responsible adult.*

Index